To

...........Harry...........

From

Joey, Geoff
and
Thomas

We hope you will enjoy
reading and learning these
prayers when you are a bit
older. God Bless You.

To John and Sara J.W.

Compiled by Lois Rock
Illustrations copyright © 2000 John Wallace
This edition copyright © 2000 Lion Hudson

The moral rights of the author and illustrator
have been asserted

A Lion Children's Book
an imprint of
Lion Hudson plc
Wilkinson House, Jordan Hill Road,
Oxford OX2 8DR, England
www.lionhudson.com
ISBN: 978-0-7459-4296-4

First UK edition 2000
10

Acknowledgments
'First the seed' by Lilian Cox. Reproduced from
New Child Songs by permission of the National
Christian Education Council.

'Summer sky of blue and white' by
Mary Joslin, 'When I am in a temper' by
Mark Robinson and 'Dear God, you are my
shepherd' by Lois Rock are copyright © Lion
Hudson.

'Dear Father, hear and bless': source unknown.

A catalogue record for this book is available
from the British Library

Typeset in 14/21 Latin725 BT
Printed in China May 2012
(manufacturer LH17)

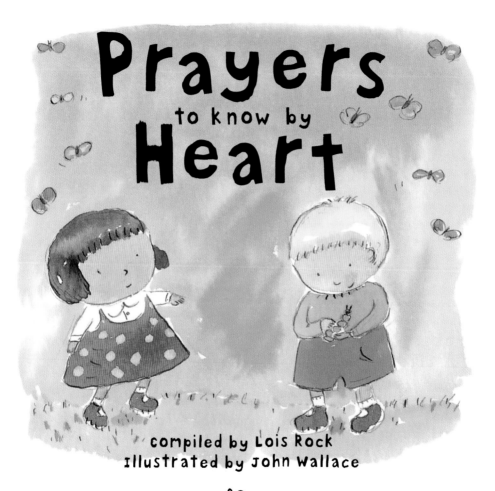

Prayers
to know by
Heart

compiled by Lois Rock
Illustrated by John Wallace

LION
CHILDREN'S

Thank you, God in heaven
For a day begun.
Thank you for the breezes,
Thank you for the sun.
For this time of gladness,
For our work and play,
Thank you, God in heaven
For another day.

Traditional

All things bright and beautiful,
All creatures great and small,
All things wise and wonderful,
The Lord God made them all.

Cecil Frances Alexander (1818–95)

Dear Father, hear and bless
Thy beasts and singing birds,
And guard with tenderness
Small things that have no words.

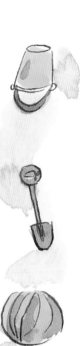

God, who made the earth,
The air, the sky, the sea,
Who gave the light its birth,
Careth for me.

God, who made the grass,
The flower, the fruit, the tree,
The day and night to pass,
Careth for me.

God, who made all things,
On earth, in air, in sea,
Who changing seasons brings,
Careth for me.

Sarah Betts Rhodes (c. 1870)

Dear God, you are my shepherd,
You give me all I need,
You take me where the grass grows green
And I can safely feed.

You take me where the water
Is quiet and cool and clear;
And there I rest and know I'm safe
For you are always near.

Lois Rock, based on Psalm 23

First the seed
And then the grain;
Thank you, God,
For sun and rain.

First the flour
And then the bread;
Thank you, God,
That we are fed.

Thank you, God,
For all your care;
Help us all
To share and share.

Lilian Cox

When I am in a temper
When I get really mad
I can be very dangerous
I can be very bad.

I'm wild as a tiger
I'm wild as a bear
I'm wilder than a wildebeest
And I don't even care.

Dear God who made the tiger
Dear God who made the bear
Please let me know you love me still
And that you'll always care.

Mark Robinson

Now I lay me down to sleep,
I pray thee, Lord, thy child to keep;
Thy love to guard me through the night
And wake me in the morning light.

Traditional

Summer sky of blue and white,
Winter sky of grey;
Pink and orange in the dawnlight,
Red at close of day;
Noontime sun of golden yellow,
Moon with silver light:
Sing with gladness for the daytime,
Give thanks for the night.

Mary Joslin

God bless all those that I love;
God bless all those that love me;
God bless all those that love those that I love
and all those that love those that love me.

From an old New England sampler

Lord, keep us safe this night,
Secure from all our fears;
May angels guard us while we sleep,
Till morning light appears.

John Leland (1754–1841)

The moon shines bright,
The stars give light
Before the break of day;
God bless you all
Both great and small
And send a joyful day.

Traditional